An Introduction to DOCKER

Table of Contents

Introduction

The Docker is a very useful software program. Most people confuse it with the VirtualBox. The two are closely related, but they are not the same. People think that the Docker is a native Virtual Machine, which is not the case. This book will help you to understand the Docker in detail, as no detail has been left out.

Most system administrators also find it difficult to run the Docker in both the Windows OS and the Mac OS X. However, this book will act as a guide for you on how to do this, and thus, you will become an expert in using the Docker in the various operating systems.

Chapter 1- Definition

The Docker is an open-source software program used by system administrators for the creation of lightweight virtual machines. However, the virtual machine in this case is not the native one, meaning that it is not more of a virtual machine. Note that the Docker can only run on Linux, but not on Windows or Mac OSX.

If you do not have Linux installed on your machine, then you should consider installing Virtual Box which will be used to run Linux. You will then be in a position to run the Docker. However, most people do not understand the real uses of the Docker. It can be used for the following purposes:

Isolating the dependencies of an application.

To provide an environment to be used to scale the instances of an application in a fast and easy manner.

For creation of an image of an application and then replicating it.

Development of applications which are ready to start and easy to distribute.

To test and dispose applications.

The Docker can be compared to the cargo container used in ships. These containers can be used on any kind of ship. Likewise, the Docker is like a container but in this case, for software applications. The container can be run on a machine, provided it has been installed with an operating system of any kind. The Docker makes it possible to separate the application from the infrastructure.

With this, it will be possible for you to treat the application like a managed application. The cycle which lies between the writing and running of code is made shorter since the Docker makes it fast to write, test, and deploy and application. With all the above, it is very clear that the Docker makes it easy to utilize the hardware very effectively so as to get the best from it.

Chapter 2 - The Architecture and Components of the Docker

The Docker is made up of two major components. These include the following:

Docker- this is the open-source container which provides us with a container for virtualization purpose.

Docker hub- this is the Software-as –a-Service platform which is used for sharing and management of the Docker containers.

The Architecture

It makes use of the client-server architecture. The client part of the DDocker communicates directly to the Docker "daemon." The daemon is responsible for heavy lifting the building, running, and then distributing the containers of the DDocker. Notice that it is possible for you to run both the Docker client and the Docker daemon on the same machine. You can also choose to connect the two remotely, in which they will be running on different and separate machines.

For the purpose of communication between the Docker client and the Docker daemon, a RESTful API or sockets are used.

Docker Daemon

You should know that the user is not allowed to directly interact with the DDocker daemon. It is run on the host machine. For the user to access or communicate with the Docker daemon, they must do so via the Docker client.

Docker Client

This provides the use with the interface for interaction purpose. This means that it forms the UI for the Docker. It links the user to the Docker daemon, meaning that it receives commands from this user and then relays them to the Docker daemon. Notice that the communication between the client and the daemon is two way. This is for the purpose of relaying user commands to the daemon or relaying response from the daemon to the user.

The inner part of the Docker is made up of three main components. These include the following:

Docker registries.

Docker images.

Docker containers.

Docker Images

This forms a template which is read-only. These images are used for the purpose of the creation of the Docker containers. With the Docker, it is easy for one to create a Docker image or just update the one which is already in existence. You also have the choice of downloading Docker images which have already been developed by other persons.

You can take an already created image, and then modify it so as to suit your needs. After the modification, you will get what is known as the "child image." To do this, there two ways which can be followed. First, you can use a file, which specifies the base image to be used and the modifications which are to be done. You can also to run the image live, and then do the modifications. It is after the modifications that you can commit the changes. Note that each of the two ways has its own merits and demerits, but it is highly recommended that you use the file.

Each of the images is associated with a unique ID, a name which is readable by humans, and a tag pair.

Docker Registries

These are responsible for holding the images. They can either be public or private, and they are the stores where you can either download or upload the images. "Docker Hub" forms the public Docker registry. Feel free to download and upload images to this hub for your use or by use by the others. You can also use the images which have been created by others. The distribution component of the Docker is the "docker registries."

A Docker container can be compared to a directory, since it is everything which is necessary for an application to run. To develop the container, we use the Docker image. It is possible for us to either start, run, stop, move, or delete the Docker containers. A single container forms a secure platform for an application. They form the component which can be run in the Docker.

How a Docker Image works

You are aware that Docker images form a read-only template from which we can create Docker containers. The Docker image is made up of a series of layers. To combine these layers into a unit image, we make use of a "union file system."

These layers are responsible for the lightweight nature of the Docker. Changing the Docker, such as updating it to a newer version, means that a new layer has been added to it. With the actual virtual machine, the whole system gets rebuilt after the update, but this is not the case here, because only a new layer gets added or the existing one gets updated. This means that when you need to distribute the image, you will only distribute the new layer which has been added, rather than distributing the whole system. This makes the process very easy and faster.

Each of the images must begin from a base image. Your own image can also be used to form the base for other images. A good example of this is the Apache image, which can be used to form the base image for all your web images. To develop the whole Docker, a set of steps normally referred to as "instructions" is followed from the base image. Each of the instructions in the set is aimed at creating a new layer for the Docker. Some of the instructions include the following:
Running a command.

Adding a directory or a file.

Creating an environmental variable.

Note that a file known as "Dockerfile" is used for storage of these instructions. Whenever you request to build an image, the instructions will be executed, and then you will get back the final image.

How a Docker Registry works

This forms the store where your images can be stored. After creating your Docker image, you can upload to the public registry which we referred to as the "Docker Hub" or upload to a private registry which runs behind your firewall.

If you need to use the images which have been created by others, just use your Docker client, and search for the images which have been already published and then download them to your Docker host. You can then use these to build your own containers.

How the Container works

The Container is made up of the files added by the user, the operating system, and the meta-data. As you know, we build the Container from the image. The image is responsible for telling the Docker what the Container has, the process which is to be run whenever the Container is being started and other data containing issues to do with configuration. The image for the Docker is also read-only. Whenever a Container is run by the Docker from the image, the union file system we saw earlier is used to add a new read-write layer on top of where the application can then run.

Under normal circumstances, the Docker client will always inform or instruct the Docker daemon to run the Container. This is done via the Docker API or by use of the Docker binary. Consider the command shown below:
docker run -i -t ubuntu /bin/bash

The above command will start the Docker container in Ubuntu. The "run" is a Docker binary which launches the Docker client, and then in turn the Docker container. The following is the minimum that the Dock client can instruct the Docker daemon to launch the Docker container:

The Docker image where the Docker Container should be built from. In the above command, we will use the Ubuntu base image.

The command to be run inside the container once it has been launched. With "/bin/bash", the Bash shell will be started inside the container.
After executing the above command, the following sequence of steps will take place:

The "Ubuntu" image will be pulled- the Docker will check whether the "Ubuntu" is available. If it is not available, then the Docker will download it from the "Docker Hub." However, if the image is already available, the Docker just directly uses for the Container, that is, the new one.

Creation of a new Container- after the image is found, it is used by the Docker for creation of a new image.

Allocation of a file system and mounting of a read-write layer- a new Container is created in the file system, and then a new layer which is read-write is added to the image.

Allocation of a network/bridge interface- we need the Docker Container to be in a position to communicate to the local interface. An interface will serve this purpose, and that is why we need it.

Setting up the IP address- an IP address is found from the pool and then attached.

The specified process is executed- at this stage, the application is run or executed.

Capturing and provision of application output- the standard input is connected and logged. Output and errors, if any, are shown so as to be sure of how the application is running.

At the last stage, the Container will have been set and ready for use. You can then run it, interact with the application, and the stop it when you are done with your task at hand.

Note that the Docker was written by use of the "Go" programming language which belongs to Google. It borrows very much from Linux kernel so as to provide the functionality discussed above.

The Namespaces

This is the technology that Docker relies on. This makes it possible for the Docker to provide the isolation workspace, which us commonly known as the "Container." After running your Container, a set of namespaces for it are created by the Docker. This is the one responsible for creating isolation as the Container runs since each of the aspects of the Container will be run in its own namespace without access to the outside. The following are some of the namespaces that are used by the Docker:

"pid" namespace- the PID stands for the "process ID." It is used for the purpose of isolating the process.

"net" namespace- this helps in management of the network interfaces.

"ipc" namespace- used to manage how IPCX resources are accessed.

"mnt" namespace- used for management of mount points.

"uts" namespace- used for isolation of the kernel and the version identifiers.

Chapter 3- Installing Docker in Arch Linux

To install the Docker in Arch Linux, we can make use of the packages in the community:

Docker-git- this is a Docker package, and it installs the latest version of Docker which has been tagged. It builds from the master branch which is current.

Docker- which is also a Docker package. It forms the normal package for the Docker.

The Dependencies

The several packages which Docker relies on are known as the Dependencies. They include the following:
Sqlite

bridge-utils

iproute2

device-mappe

lxc

Performing the Installation

We now need to discuss the process of installing the Docker in Arch Linux. If the installation is to be done from the normal package, then the following simple command can be used:

sudo pacman -S docker

If the installation is to be done from the AUR package, then execute the following command:

sudo yaourt -S docker-git

Note that we have assumed that you have already installed "yaourt" in your system. If not, kindly do so before starting to install the Docker.

How to start the Docker

Once you have installed the Docker in your machine running Arch Linux, you need to start it so as to begin using it. During the installation, a "system" service for the Docker was created. Run the following command so as to start the Docker:

sudo systemctl start docker

If you need to start it on system boot, run the following command:

sudo systemctl enable docker

The above are the two ways that you can start the Docker.

It is possible that you might need to add an HTTP proxy to your Docker. To do this, you can either partition the runtime files for the Docker or set a directory which is different. There are also some customizations which you can perform so as to achieve this.

How to Uninstall the Docker from Arch Linux

There might come a time when you want to uninstall the Docker, particularly when you have achieved what you wanted. To do this, just run the following command:

sudo pacman -R docker

If you need to uninstall the Docker package together with all the Dependencies which are not necessary, then use the following command:

sudo pacman -Rns docker

Note that with the above commands, the volumes, containers, images, and files which have been configured by the user will not be removed. To delete these, just execute the following command:

rm -rf /var/lib/docker

Configuration files which have been created by the user should be manually deleted.

Chapter 4- Installing Docker in Ubuntu

The following Ubuntu Operating Systems support the Docker:
Ubuntu Saucy 13.10

Ubuntu Precise 12.04 (LTS)

Ubuntu Trusty 14.04 (LTS)
In this chapter, we will use the Docker-managed release packages so as to install it in Ubuntu. Once you have used these packages for installation, you will have the latest release of the Docker. To perform the installation using Ubuntu-managed packages, consult with the Ubuntu documentation.

Requirements

Regardless of the version of Ubuntu that you are using on your machine, a 64-bit installation of the Docker will be required. Also, the minimum version of the kernel which is supported is 3.10. Newer versions which are easy to maintain are also supported. Note that kernels which are lower than 3.10 do not have the features which are necessary for the kernel to run. They also have bugs, which are errors, and these will normally lead to frequent loss of data and panic under certain circumstances.

If you need to know the version of the kernel running on your system, just open the command prompt, and then run the following command:

uname −r

In my case, I am getting the following output from the above command:

```
3.11.0-15-generic
```

From the figure above, it is clear that the version of my kernel is above 3.10. I can then safely install and run the Docker.

If your machine is running Ubuntu Precise, then the Docker will require the kernel to be version 3.13. This means that if the kernel is older than this, you will have to upgrade it. If this is the case, then follow these steps so as to do the upgrade and install newly available packages:

Login to your host, and then open the terminal.

Run the following command so as to update the package manager:

sudo apt-get update

Use the following command to install the packages, both optional and the required ones:

sudo apt-get install linux-image-generic-lts-trusty

The installation will depend on your host. Some hosts will require more packages to be installed than others.

Use the following command so as to reboot the host:

sudo reboot

After rebooting the system, continue to install the Docker.

The default storage backend for the Docker is AUFS. If it is not already installed in your system, then you need not worry because the Docker installation process will just install it for you.

The Installation Process

Before beginning the installation, you should ensure that you have all the prerequisites which we have discussed already installed. After that, you can then begin to install the Docker as follows:

Login to the system with the "sudo" privileges, that is, as a sudo (super user do) user.

Use the following command to check on whether "wget" has been installed on your system:

which wget
If you find that it is not installed, update the manager and then install it. This is shown below:

sudo apt-get update
sudo apt-get install wget

Obtain the latest image of the Docker. Use the following command:

wget -qO- https://get.docker.com/ | sh

The system will prompt you to provide the "sudo" password. Just do that. The Docker and its Dependencies will then be downloaded and installed on your system. You need to be knowledgeable about the key if your company is using one.

After the process is over, verify that the Docker has been installed. Use the following command:

sudo docker run hello-world

The above command will download a test image, which will then be run on the Container.

Additions Docker Configurations in Ubuntu

You now have the Docker installed on your system. However, there are some additional configurations which are necessary for the Docker to work better in Ubuntu. These are the configurations to be discussed.

Creating a Docker Group

The daemon for the Docker is linked to a UNIX socket, rather than to a TCP port. The "Root" user is the default owner of the UNIX socket. Other users must use the "sudo" command so as to access this socket. This is why you have to run the daemon for the Docker as the "root" user.

However, the use of the "sudo" command each time that we want to run the Docker is tiresome and also boring. We need to avoid this. To do this, you need to create UNIX group and give it the name "docker." You should then add users to this group.

When the Docker daemon is started, the ownership of this file will be made read/writable for the users in the "docker" file. This shows that the group is the same or equivalent to the "root" user.

To create the "docker" file and add users to it, follow the steps below:

Log into the system running Ubuntu with the "sudo" privileges. However, you can also follow the step below so as to achieve this privilege.

Log into the system as "Ubuntu" user. Create the group and name it "docker." Add your user to this group.

Log out of the system, and then log in again.

This is for ensuring that you are logged in with the necessary permissions.

Run the Docker with the "sudo" command so as to verify that your work was successful.

docker run hello-world

Adjusting the Memory and Swap Accounting

When working with the Docker on some systems, the user will always see some warning messages. It is possible for us to avoid or do away with these messages. This can be done by enabling memory and swap accounting on the system.

If the system is running GNU GRUB and you need to enable this, just do the following:

Log into the system but with the "sudo" privileges.

Open the file "/etc/default/grub" and then edit it.

The value for "GRUB_CMDLINE_LINUX" should be set to the following:

GRUB_CMDLINE_LINUX="cgroup_enable=memory swapaccount=1"
Save the file, and then close it.
Update the "GRUB" as follows:

sudo update-grub

Finally, reboot the system.
How to enable UFW forwading

If UFW (Uncomplicated Firewall) is being used on the same host that the Docker is running, then an additional configuration needs to be done. The Docker normally uses a container bridge for the purpose of managing networking. By default, this firewall prevents the process of forwarding of traffic.

This means that you have to reconfigure this setting about the UFW's forwarding policy. By default, the UFW will block any traffic which is incoming. This means that to be able to get traffic from other containers, you must configure the Docker port number 2375 to allow this.

This can be done as follows:

Log into the system running Ubuntu with "sudo" privileges.

Verify whether the firewall has been installed and enabled by use of the following command:

sudo ufw status

We now need to edit the file "/etc/default/ufw" for editing purpose. Open it as follows:

sudo nano /etc/default/ufw

Edit the "DEFAULT_FORWARD_POLICY" and set it to the following:

DEFAULT_FORWARD_POLICY="ACCEPT"

Save the changes, and then close the file.

To apply the new changes to the UFW, just restart it as follows:

sudo ufw reload

We now need to make the port number 2375 allow incoming traffic into the container. This can be done by use of the following command:

sudo ufw allow 2375/tcp

The Docker will then have been set.
Configuring the DNS Server to be used by the Docker

Systems running either Ubuntu or a derivative of the same on their desktop will use the IP address 127.0.0.1 as their name server, whose configuration is in the file "/etc/resolv.conf." The NetworkManager will also set up "dnsmasq" for using the real DNS servers of the established connection and the nameserver will be set to 127.0.0l1 in the above file we have mentioned.

If these configurations are being set on the machine on which you are running the Docker, you will always see the following warning whenever you are starting up:

WARNING: Local (127.0.0.1) DNS resolver found in resolv.conf and containers

can't use it. Using default external servers : [8.8.8.8 8.8.4.4]

The cause of the failure is because it is not able to use the local DNS as the nameserver. It will then shift and use an external nameserver. If you need to do away with the warning, you can configure the nameserver that the Docker containers should use. You can also avoid this by disabling "dnsmasq," which can be found in the NetworkManager. However, you need to be careful when doing this as it makes the process of DNS resolution slow depending on the kind of network that you are using.

If you need to specify the DNS server which is to be used by the Docker, follow the steps below:

Log into the system running Ubuntu with "sudo" privileges.

We now need to open the file "/etc/default/docker" for editing. Open it by running the following command:

sudo nano /etc/default/docker

Change the following Docker setting:

DOCKER_OPTS="--dns 8.8.8.8"

You should change the "8.8.8.8" to your local DNS server such as "192.168.160.1." If you have multiple of the DNS servers, then feel free to specify them. Note that the DNS servers should be separated with spaces as shown below:

--dns 8.8.8.8 --dns 192.168.160.1

For those who are using laptops which are connected to numerous networks,   and then set the DNS server to public. You can then save the changes made to the file, and then close it.

The Dicker daemon should then be restarted by use of the following command:

sudo restart docker

We also said that the above can be achieved by disabling the "dnsmasq" which can be found in the NetworkManager. However, this can make your network a bit slow. It can be done as follows:

We need to open the file
"/etc/NetworkManager/NetworkManager.conf" for editing.
Use the following command to open it:
sudo nano /etc/NetworkManager/NetworkManager.conf
In the file, find "dns=dsnmasq" and then comment it out.

dns=dnsmasq

Save the changes, and then close the file.
Use the following commands to restart both the Docker and the NetworkManager:

sudo restart network-manager
 sudo restart docker

Upgrading the Docker

It is possible that you might need to upgrade the Docker which is running on your Ubuntu system. In this case, we use "wget" as shown below:

```
wget -qO- https://get.docker.com/ | sh
```

Uninstalling the Docker

Once you are done with what you were doing with the Docker, you might need to uninstall it. To uninstall the package for the Docker, just use the command shown below:

sudo apt-get purge lxc-docker

To install both the Docker package and the Dependencies which are not necessary, then use the following command:

sudo apt-get autoremove --purge lxc-docker

Note that with the two commands shown above, the images, volumes, containers, and configuration files created by the user will not be deleted. To delete all of these, kindly use the following command:

rm -rf /var/lib/docker

The command will delete all of the above, including containers, images, and volumes. However, in the case of the configuration files which have been created by the user, you will have to delete them manually.

Chapter 5- Installing the Docker Engine on Windows

The Docker engine uses features which are specific to the Linux-kernel. If you need to run it on a Windows machine, then you will need a lightweight virtual machine (VM). For us to control the Docker Engine which has been virtualized for building, running, and managing the Docker containers, we use the "Windows Docker Client."

There are some applications which are available for free download online, and these will assist you to create a Linux Virtual Machine on your Windows computer, and you will be in a position to run the Docker.

Note that you will be using the Windows Docker Client, but the Docker engine housing the containers will be running on the Linux OS. If the Docker engine for Windows was available, you could only run Linux containers from the Windows machine.

The Installation process

Go online, and find the latest release of "Docker Client for Windows Installer" and then download it.

Once the download is over, just run it. This will install the Docker Client for Windows, Git for Windows, VirtualBox, Boot2Docker management toll, and the boot2docker Linux ISO.

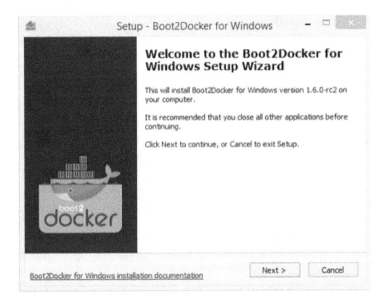

Navigate to the desktop of your machine, find the "Boot2Docker Start" shortcut, and then click on it to run it. If you fail to find it on the Desktop, navigate to "Program Files → Boot2Docker for Windows" and you will find it. By default, you will be asked to provide the Ssh key Passphrase. Just hit the "Enter" key, and all will be well. However, this is not very secure.

A Unix shell will be started by the "Boot2Docker Start," and this will already have been configured so as to manage the Docker, which is running on a virtual machine. If you need to check whether this is happening, just run the command "docker version."

```
ahmetb@ALP-HP ~
$ docker version
Client version: 1.6.0-rc2
Client API version: 1.18
Go version (client): go1.4.2
Git commit (client): c5ee149
OS/Arch (client): windows/amd64
Server version: 1.6.0-rc2
Server API version: 1.18
Go version (server): go1.4.2
Git commit (server): c5ee149
OS/Arch (server): linux/amd64

ahmetb@ALP-HP ~
$ _
```

How to Run the Docker

If the Docker daemon that you are using to run your system is remote, then avoid using the "sudo" keyword before your commands as we have been doing in the previous chapters.

With the Boot2Docker start, a shell with environment variables which have already been set will be started. This means that you will just have to start using the Docker. Let us try to check if the system is ready to be used by testing the image:

docker run hello-world

Just run the command shown above. What the command does is that it will download an "hell-world" image and it will then print a message saying "Hello from Docker."

How to use the Docker from the Windows Command Prompt

Begin by launching or starting the command prompt of the Windows OS.
For the Bit2Docker, the "ssh.exe" is needed to be set in the path. This explains the need for inclusion of the "bin" folder of the installation of Git to the "%PATH%" which is an environmental path. This can be done by running the following command:

set PATH=%PATH%;"c:\Program Files (x86)\Git\bin"

```
c:\>set PATH=%PATH%;"c:\Program Files (x86)\Git\bin"

c:\>boot2docker start
Waiting for VM and Docker daemon to start...
..........ooo
Started.
```

After running the previous command, we then need to start the Boot2Docker VM by running the following command:

boot2docker start
However, at this stage, you might get an error telling you that the machine doesn't exist. To solve this, run the following command:

boot2dockerinit
After that, you can then copy and paste the commands for setting the environment variable on the cmd.exe. You will then be ready to run the Docker commands.

How to use the Docker from PowerShell

Begin by starting the PowerShell window. After that, you can add "ssh.exe" to the Path. This can be done by use of the command shown below:

$Env:Path = "${Env:Path};c:\Program Files (x86)\Git\bin"

After the above command, just run the command "boot2docker start." The command will print all the PowerShell commands necessary for setting environment variables which are needed for connection of a Docker which is running in a virtual machine. After the above commands, you will be ready and set to run other Docker commands.

```
PS C:\> $Env:Path = "${Env:Path};c:\Program Files (x86)\Git\bin"
PS C:\> boot2docker start
Waiting for VM and Docker daemon to start...
........oo
Started.
```

However, you might not be interested in the idea of copying and pasting on the Power Shell. If this is the case, then you can set the environment variable by running the command "boot2docker shellinit | Invoke-Expression."

How to Upgrade the Docker

Remember we said that to upgrade the Docker, a new layer is added on top of the already existing layers. To do this, follow the steps below:

Find the latest release of the "Docker for Windows Installer" and then download it on your machine.

You can then run the Installer. What will happen is that the Boot2Docker management tool will be updated.

It is now time to upgrade the virtual machine which exists. To do this, open the terminal, and then run the following command:

```
boot2docker stop
boot2docker download
boot2docker start
```

How to redirect the Container port

The boot2docker has a default username of "docker" and a password of "tcuser." It is good for you to know that.

If the boot2docker is of the latest version, it will set up a network adapter which is host only and this will provide access to the ports of the container.
Running a container whose port is exposed:

docker run --rm -i -t -p 80:80 nginx

After running the above command, you should then be in apposition to access the nginx server by use of the IP address that you were informed to use. This will be as follows:

boot2docker ip

In most cases, the value of the IP address is "192.168.59.103." However, it is possible for this to get changed by the DHCP implementation of the virtualbox.

How to use PUTTY rather than the CMD to login

What the boot2docker does is that it generates a private/public key combination in the directory "%USERPROFILE%\.ssh."To login, you will need to use the private key which you can get from the above mentioned directory.

However, the format of the key will not be supported by PUTTY. This means that you to convert it into a format which is supportable by PUTTY. Puttygen can be used for this purpose. To do this, follow the steps given below:

Launch "puttygen.exe." You can then load the private key, that is, "File->Load."The loading should be done from "%USERPROFILE%\.ssh\id_boot2docker."

Save the key by clicking on "Save Private Key."

The saved file should then be used to log im with the private key. The following command should be used:

docker@127.0.0.1:2022

How to uninstall Boot2docker

To uninstall this in Windows, just follow the usual way of uninstalling other software and applications. Just open the command prompt and click on the "uninstall a program" link. On the window which appears, just look for the Boot2ckjer and then uninstall it. However, you need to know that the file "docker-install.exe" will not be removed by use of this procedure. You will have to manually delete it.

Chapter 6- Installing Docker in Mac OS X

Again, to install the Docker on this OS, we must use the Boot2Docker. We will then be in a position to run the Docker commands on the command line. If you are an expert in using the command prompt, then this is the best installation method for you. It also suits those who want to make a contribution on Github to the Docker project.

It is also recommended that you use kitematic. With this, you will be in a position to set up the Docker on your machine, and then run it via a GUI (Graphical User Interface).

Command-line Docker with Boot2Docker

You are very aware that the Docker relies highly on features which are related to the Linux-kernel. Linux and OS X are two different operating systems. This means that we cannot directly install and run the Docker on Mac OS X. To solve this problem, we must first install the Boot2Docker application. This application comes with the Docker itself, a virtual box, and the Boot2Docker management tool.

The Boot2Docker management tool is like a lightweight virtual machine which is solely based on Linux and it enables us to run the Docker daemon on the OS X for Mac. The VirtualBox VM is very small, approximately 24MB in size, and it takes a very short time for it to get booted, approximately five seconds.

The Requirements

The Mac machine that you are using should be installed with OS X 10.6 "Snow Leopard" or a newer version of this so that it can be able to support the Boot2Docker.

Key concepts

When installing the Docker on Linux, you must have noticed that it is both the Docker host and the localhost. In the field of networking, the localhost represents your own computer. The Docker host is represented by the machine on which the container is running.

When using Linux OS on your machine, the Docker daemon, the Docker client, and the other containers directly run on the localhost. This is an indication that the Docker ports on the container can be addressed. In this case, we will use the standard addressing of the localhost such as the one shown below:

0.0.0.0:8376 or localhost:8000

In the case of the Mac OS X, this is totally different. The Docker daemon in this case will be running inside the virtual machine for Linux which is provided by the Boot2Docker. This means that the address of the Linux virtual machine will be used as the address of the Docker host. When the boot2docker process is started, then the Linux virtual machine will be assigned an IP address. You will understand this in detail as this chapter continues.

The process of Installation

Open the page for "boot2docker/osx-installer".

Navigate to the "Downloads" section and the click on "Boot2Docker-x.x.x.pkg." This will download the Boot2Docker for you.

Double-click on the downloaded package so as to install the boot2docker.

The Boot2Docker and the Virtual machine will be placed in the "Applications" folder by the installer. The boot2docker and the Docker binaries will be placed in the "/usr/local/bin" directory by the installation process.

Starting the Boot2Docker Application

For you to be able to run the Docker container, you must begin by running the boot2docker VM. It is after this that you can run the Docker commands for loading, creating and managing containers. To launch the boot2docker, you can choose to do it from the command line or from the Applications folder.

However, you need to note that boot2docker was designed for the purpose of development, so you should not use it in a production environment.

Launching from the Applications folder

When you launch or start the boot2docker from this Docker, the application will do the following:
Open a terminal window.

Create a directory named "$HOME/.boot2docker."

Create virtualbox certs and ISO.

The virtual box machine running the Docker daemon will be started.
Once the whole application is started or launched, you can then begin to run or execute the Docker commands. If you need to test or check whether your installation of the app was successful, just download and run the "hello-word" test app. The following command should be run for this purpose:

docker run hello-world

This will download and run the app on your Docker container. You will see the "Hello world" message on the Docker container.

```
$ docker run hello-world
Unable to find image 'hello-world:latest' locally
511136ea3c5a: Pull complete
31cbccb51277: Pull complete
e45a5af57b00: Pull complete
hello-world:latest: The image you are pulling has been verified.
Important: image verification is a tech preview feature and should not be
relied on to provide security.
Status: Downloaded newer image for hello-world:latest
Hello from Docker.
This message shows that your installation appears to be working correctly.
```

The most recommended way to start and stop the boot2docker on your machine is to use the command line.

From the command line

If you need to initialize and run boot2docker from your command line, then follow the steps below:

Create a Boot2Docker VM, that is, a new one. Use the command given below for this purpose:

boot2docker init

The command needs to be run only once, and it will create a virtual machine for you.

You can the launch the boot2docker Virtual Machine. Use the command given below:

boot2docker start

You can then display the environment variables which belong to the Docker client. Use the following command:
boot2docker shellinit

Note that the specific address and paths on the machine will not be the same.

If you need to set the environment variables in your shell, then execute the following command:

eval "$(boot2docker shellinit)"

You can also choose to do this manually. To do this, use the "export" commands which have been returned by the "boot2docker".

Verify the setup by running the "hello-world" container. The following command should be used for this:

docker run hello-world

By now, the boot2docker should be running on your system. The Docker client should also be already initialized. If you need to verify these, then run the following commands:

```
boot2docker status
docker version
```

How to Access the Container ports

To do this, follow the steps below:
On the DOCKER_HOST, start the NGINX container. Use the following command:

docker run -d -P --name web nginx

In normal circumstances, when the command "docker run" is executed, the container will be started, run, and then it will exit. The use of the "-d" flag will cause the container to run in the background after the "docker run" command completes its execution. With the "-p" flag, the ports which are exposed will be published from the container to the localhost. They will then be accessible from your Mac.

Use the "docker ps" container to display the running container. The ID of the container, its image, and the command will be displayed. After the display, you will notice that the "nginx" will be running as a daemon.

View just the ports of the container. Just use the following command:

docker port web

In my case, the above command gives me the following output:

```
443/tcp -> 0.0.0.0:49156

80/tcp -> 0.0.0.0:49157
```

From the above figure, it is clear that the port number 80 of the "web" container has been mapped to port number49157 on the Docker host.

On your browser, enter the IP address "http://localhost:49157". Note that the address for the localhost is "0.0.0.0".

You will notice that the address will not work. The reason is because the DOCKER_HOST address has not been set to the localhost address which is (0.0.0.0). Instead of using this, we have used the address of the boot2docker Virtual Machine.

You should then obtain the boot2docker Virtual Machine address. This can be done by use of the following command:

boot2docker ip

At this point, clearly mark the address that you get as the output of the above command.

Open your browser, and provide the following the following IP URL: http://IP:49157, where IP is the address that you get after running the above command. After providing the URL and hitting the "Enter" key, you will be taken to the home page for "NGINX." This is shown in the figure below:

If you see the above window, just known that you are successful.

Note that at this time, "Nginx" is up and running. You might need to stop and then remove the running nginx container. This can be done by use of the following commands:

```
docker stop web
docker rm web
```

Mount a volume on container

When the boot2docker is launched, it will normally share the directory b"/Users" with the Virtual Machine (VM). If you need to mount directories onto a container, then this book will guide you on how to do it. To mount the volume on a container, kindly follow the steps below:

Navigate to your "$HOME" directory. This can be done with the following command:

cd $HOME

Make a new directory for the "site.". This can be done as follows:

mkdir site

Navigate to the above created directory, that is, the "site" directory. Use the command shown below:

cd site

Create a new file and name it "index.html." Use the following command to do this:

echo "New site" > index.html

Launch a new "nginx" container and then replace the "html" folder with the directory of your site. This can be done as follows:

docker run -d -P -v $HOME/site:/usr/share/nginx/html -- name newsite nginx

Obtain the port of the "newsite" container. Just use the following command:

docker port newsite

You can then use the browser to open the site. Use the address that you get above. The site will be as follows:

new site

Try to add a new page to your site. This should be done in real time in the directory "HOME/site." Consider the command shown below:

echo "This site is a nice one" > nice.html

Once you have added the page above, open it in the browser. This is shown in the figure below:

This site is a nice one

You can then stop, and the running "newsite" container should be removed. This can be accomplished by use of the following commands:

docker stop newsite
docker rm newsite

How to upgrade the Boot2Docker

For those using Boot2Docker 1.4.1 or greater, it is possible for you to use the command line so as to update this. For those using an older version of this, use the package which the boot2docker repository provides.
Using the Command line

If you need to upgrade boot2docker 1.4.q or greater via the command line, following the procedure below:

Log into your local machine and then open its terminal.

Stop the running boot2docker application using the following command:

boot2docker stop

Execute the upgrade command as shown below:

boot2docker upgrade

Using the Installer

Any version of boot2docker can be upgraded as follows:

Log into your local machine and then open the terminal.

Stop the running boot2docker application by use of the following command:

boot2docker stop

Navigate to the webpage for "boot2docker/osx-installer".

Click on the link written "Boot2Docker-x.x.x.pkg" so as to download the boot2docker. This can be found in the "Downloads" section of the web page.

Double click on the downloaded package so as to install the boot2docker. The "boot2docker" will be placed in the "Applications" folder by the installer.

Uninstalling the Boot2Docker

To do this, follow the steps given below:
Navigate to the webpage for "boot2docker/osx-installer."
Navigate to the "Downloads" section of the web page, and then click on "Source code (tar.gz)" or "Source code (zip)." This will download the source code for you.
Extract the downloaded source code.
On your local machine, open the terminal.
Change the directory to where you did the extraction of the source code. This is shown below:
cd <path leading to the extracted source code>

Make the script "uninstall.sh" executable. This is shown below:

chmod +x uninstall.sh

Execute the above script as shown below:

./uninstall.sh

Conclusion

It can be concluded that the Docker is an open-source software which is used by system administrators for the development of lightweight virtual machines. Most people think that the Docker is a native virtual machine, but this is not the case. The fact is that it offers functionalities which are close to those offered by virtual machines.

Note that the Docker relies on features which are solely based on Linux. This explains why it is impossible for system administrators to run it on a native Windows OS or the native Mac OS X. To run the Docker on these operating systems, we need to begin by installing the "Boot2Docker" which offers a virtualization environment. This means that we will be in a position to run the Linux OS on top of either the Windows OS or the Mac OS X. The Docker offers numerous functionalities which have been discussed in this book.

Installing the Docker on the various operating systems involves different steps. This means that you should understand how to do it on the operating system that you are using on your machine. During the process of upgrading the Docker, new layers are added to the already existing layers. This makes it easy for system administrators to distribute the Docker if needed.